HOW IT HAPPENS
at the Building Site

By Jenna Anderson
Photographs by Bob and Diane Wolfe

CLARA HOUSE BOOKS

Minneapolis

The publisher would like to thank Christian Builders, Inc., and its employees for their generous help with this book.

All photographs by Bob and Diane Wolfe except pp. 1 (Photodisc), 3 (Christian Builders, Inc.), 13 (Christian Builders, Inc.), 31 (Christian Builders, Inc.), and back cover (Photodisc).

Clara House Books
The Oliver Press, Inc.
Charlotte Square
5707 West 36th Street
Minneapolis, MN 55416-2510

Library of Congress Cataloging-in-Publication Data
Anderson, Jenna, 1977-
    How it happens at the building site / by Jenna Anderson ; photographs by Bob and Diane Wolfe.
        p. cm.
    ISBN 1-881508-95-1
    1. House construction—Juvenile literature. I. Title: At the building site. II. Wolfe, Robert L.
    III. Wolfe, Diane. IV. Title.

TH4811.5.A6 2004
690'.837—dc22

                                                    2004043910

ISBN 1-881508-95-1
Printed in the United States of America
10 09 08 07 06 05 04   8 7 6 5 4 3 2 1

Imagine yourself standing in the living room of your brand-new home. You can smell the fresh paint, feel the soft carpet, and watch the fire blazing in the fireplace. It seems hard to believe, but only a few months ago this was a busy construction site. The shouts of workers, the pounding of hammers, and the smell of sawdust filled the air. How did a finished house come from all that noisy activity?

Building a house is a long and complex process. It takes many types of workers, including carpenters, roofers, electricians, and plumbers. This book will show how all these people work together to build a house from the ground up.

Surveying

The first step in building a house is defining the edges of the **lot**. The lot is the piece of land the house will stand on, along with the yard around it. The next step is figuring out where to place the house. Laws say that houses need to be a certain distance away from roads and other buildings.

Both these jobs are done by workers called **surveyors**. Plans like this one tell them the size and shape of the house.

The surveyors use a special tool called a **total station** to measure distances and angles so they can mark out the edges of the house and lot.

Foundation

Workers use a **backhoe** (left) and a **bulldozer** to dig a hole where the house will be.

Inside the hole, workers build the **foundation** that will support the house. Wet **concrete** is poured into forms to make the **footings**, or base, for the house. Then workers make walls out of lightweight concrete bricks called **cinder blocks**.

A worker called a **mason** uses a **trowel** to spread **mortar** (wet concrete) on top of the cinder blocks. The mortar makes the blocks stick together.

8

There is a space between the edge of the hole and the walls so masons and other workers can move around. After they finish the foundation, a bulldozer fills in the space with dirt.

Framing

Next, carpenters build the **frame** of the house—the wooden walls, floor, and ceiling.

The frame is like the skeleton of the house. As the frame is built, you can begin to see the shape of the house. The green covering over the frame helps protect the wood from wind and rain.

Roofing

Workers nail shingles to the top of the house. Shingles protect the roof from rain and snow.

Plumbing, Heating, and Cooling

The water most people use for drinking and washing comes from a central supply. It enters each house through a main pipe and then travels in smaller pipes to sinks, bathtubs, and other places where it is needed.

Here, a plumber installs some of these pipes. He uses a **blowtorch** (right) to melt **solder** (SOD-er), a soft metal that will act as a glue to hold the pipes together.

The sinks, showers, and toilets are all hooked up to the plumbing system. This worker is putting in the shower stall.

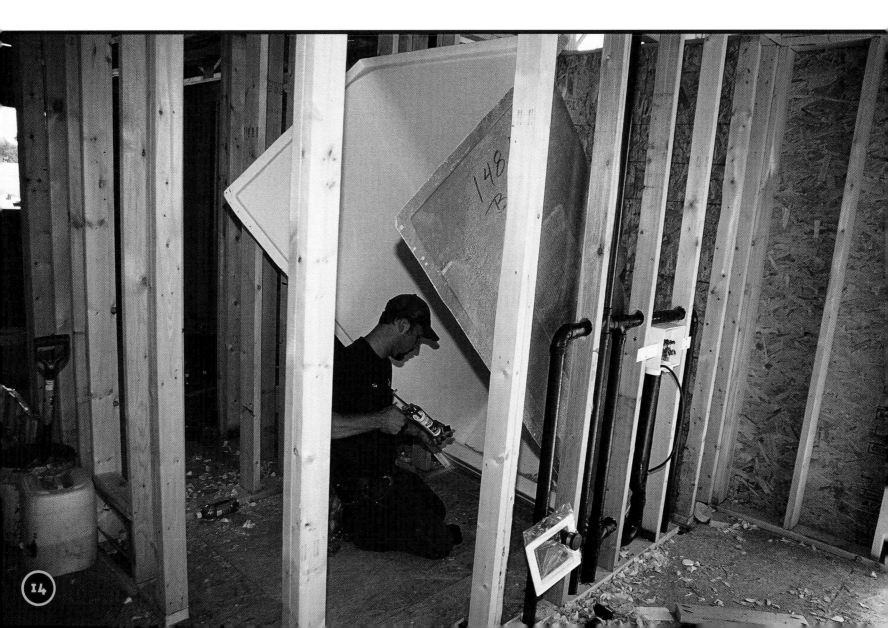

Another part of the plumbing system is the water heater. This large tank warms, stores, and supplies hot water.

The house's heating and cooling system is also installed at this time. Here, a worker connects **ducts** that will carry air in and out of the furnace and air conditioner.

Electric

Each work crew has a set of plans designed especially for its job. These electricians use their plans to figure out where the wiring, outlets, and light fixtures will go.

Wires that will carry electricity through the house are installed in the walls.

Walls and Insulation

Next, a worker fills the walls with insulation. The insulation helps keep the house warm in the winter and cool in the summer.

To finish the walls and ceilings, the workers cover the frame with sheets of **drywall**—special boards made of paper and plaster.

The cracks between the sheets of drywall are filled in (top). Then the walls are sanded down to make them smooth. These workers stand on stilts to reach the high places.

Siding

Meanwhile, workers cover the outside of the house with siding. The siding is like skin that protects the house from the weather. Houses can be covered in a variety of materials, such as wood, brick, or aluminum. This house's siding is made of vinyl, a kind of plastic.

Woodwork

Finishing touches are also being put on the inside of the house. These carpenters are making and installing wooden **trim**, including the railing that runs along the staircase.

Another worker puts in the kitchen cabinets.

Paint

Now the walls and ceilings are painted. The painters use rollers like these to cover large areas quickly.

Smaller, more detailed areas like this one need to be painted with brushes.

Lighting

Other finishing touches include light fixtures, like the ceiling fan being installed here.

Flooring

Houses can have many different kinds of floor coverings. Some of the most common are linoleum, tile, carpet, and wood. This house will have tile in the entryway. A worker prepares the area by spreading a special **cement**.

Tiles are glued down after the cement dries. The spaces between the tiles will be filled with a special kind of cement called **grout**.

Other steps in finishing the house include **varnishing** the woodwork, adding appliances, and installing hardware such as doorknobs.

Finally, it is time for the new owners to move in and make this house a home.

Glossary

backhoe: a machine used for digging large holes

blowtorch: a hand-held flame used for soldering

bulldozer: a large machine used for clearing and smoothing land

cement: a building material made out of clay and water mixed together and then hardened

cinder blocks: lightweight concrete blocks

concrete: a hard, strong material made up of sand and gravel and held together with cement

drywall: special boards made of paper and plaster

ducts: tubes that carry hot and cold air throughout a house

footings: the concrete base of a house; part of the foundation

foundation: the structure that supports the house

frame: the wooden walls, floors, and ceilings that make up the skeleton of the house

grout: a type of cement used to fill in spaces between tiles

lot: the piece of land the house stands on, along with the yard around it

mason: a person who works with stone or brick

mortar: wet concrete used to bind bricks together

solder: a soft metal that is melted and used as a glue to hold other metals together

surveyors: workers who figure out where the edges of a lot are

total station: a special tool used by surveyors to measure distances and angles

trim: finishing touches in a house, such as railings and mantels

trowel: a hand tool used for spreading cement or concrete

varnish: a special kind of paint that gives wood a clear, glossy finish